Food

In Grandma's Day

by Valerie Weber
and Jeraldine Jackson

Carolrhoda Books, Inc./Minneapolis

Carolrhoda Books, Inc., A Division of the Lerner Publishing Group
241 First Avenue North, Minneapolis, MN 55401 U.S.A.

Website address: www.lernerbooks.com

Planning and production by Discovery Books
Edited by Faye Gardner
Text designed by Ian Winton
Illustrations by Stuart Lafford
Commissioned photography by Sabine Beaupré and Jim Wend

The publishers would like to thank Jeraldine Jackson for her help in the preparation of this book.

Library of Congress Cataloging-in-Publication Data

Weber, Valerie.
  Food in Grandma's day / by Valerie Weber and Jeraldine Jackson.
     p.   cm. — (In Grandma's day)
  Includes index.
  Summary: Recalls what it was like for a young African American girl to help prepare meals for her large family living in Madison, Illinois, in the 1930s and 1940s.
  ISBN 1-57505-328-4 (alk. paper)
  1. Afro-American cookery—History—Juvenile literature. 2. Afro-Americans—Social life and customs—Juvenile literature. 3. Afro-Americans—Food—Juvenile literature. 4. Jackson, Jeraldine, 1932-   —Biography—Juvenile literature. [1. Food habits—History—20th century. 2. Jackson, Jeraldine, 1932-   —Childhood and youth. 3. Afro-Americans—Biography.] I. Jackson, Jeraldine, 1932-   . II. Title. III. Series: Weber, Valerie. In Grandma's day.
TX715.W367   1999   98-10184
641.59'296073—dc21

Printed in Hong Kong
Bound in the United States of America
1 2 3 4 5 6 - OS - 04 03 02 01 00 99

Contents

Feeding a Big Family   4

Mama Lou   6

My Responsibilities   8

A Different Kitchen   10

Rationing for War   12

Digging for Victory   14

Canning: A Family Event   16

Storing the Fruits of Summer   18

Breakfast   20

Grandma's Great Food   22

Homework and Cleaning Up   24

Neighborhood Shopping   26

Homemade Treats   28

Glossary   30

For Further Reading   31

Index   32

Feeding a Big Family

Hi! My name is Jeraldine Jackson. I have six kids and eleven grandchildren, ages four to twenty-one. Here you can see me with Jarred, who is seven years old, and Janay, who is four.

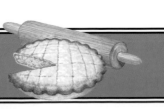

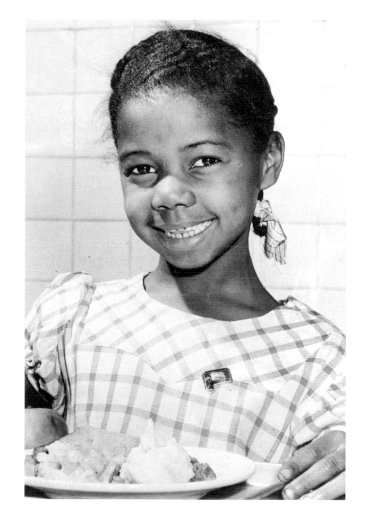

I was born in 1932 and grew up in Madison, Illinois, across the Mississippi River from St. Louis, Missouri. I was the fourth of eleven children—six girls and five boys. Big families were common when I grew up in the 1930s and 1940s. What was unusual were families with only one or two children. I knew several families with sixteen kids. That's a lot of mouths to feed!

The way we lived and the food we cooked might be somewhat similar to the way you and your family live and cook. But you might be surprised at some things we did differently.

Mama Lou

We lived in a duplex, which we called an "up-and-down," in the "colored" section of town. ("Colored" was what African Americans were called for a long time in this country.) Right next door lived my mother's mother, Lou. She spent little time at her own home, since she was always cooking, cleaning, sewing, and doing many things for us over at our house. She was there when we woke up in the morning until we went to bed at night. We called her Mama.

My grandmother did not waste a thing; everything was used and reused. We were poor, but we didn't know it, since everyone around us had just what we had. Mama would make biscuits out of lard from a five-gallon can. Then she made any leftover biscuits into bread pudding with raisins.

Nobody could make bread pudding with hot lemon sauce like my grandma. Here's her recipe:

Bread Pudding and Lemon Sauce

- 2 1/4 pounds slightly stale bread or biscuits cut into 3/4-inch cubes
- 1 cup raisins
- 1 large can pineapple pieces
- 1 cup butter
- 6 cups whole milk
- 1 1/4 cups sugar
- 1 1/2 teaspoons ground cinnamon
- 8 eggs, beaten
- 2 teaspoons vanilla extract

Grease 9- by 13-inch pan with solid vegetable shortening. Preheat oven to 350°. Combine bread cubes, raisins, and pineapple chunks in large bowl and mound into prepared pan. Bread should be piled 2 to 3 inches over top of pan. Over medium heat, melt butter in milk. Add sugar and cinnamon and let cool. Add eggs and vanilla and mix well.   Pour liquid over bread cubes and press well to be sure bread soaks up all liquid. Bread should be level with pan. Bake for 45 minutes. Remove from oven and let cool slightly, then cut into 12 to 16 pieces and put in bowls. Spoon warm sauce over each serving.

- 1 cup butter
- 2 cups sugar
- 1 tablespoon cornstarch
- juice from 1 lemon
- 1 cup half-and-half

Melt butter in heavy saucepan. Add sugar and cornstarch and stir until dissolved. Add half-and-half and bring to boil. Remove from heat and let cool slightly. Add lemon and stir. Serve warm.

My big sister, Eleanor, got married at seventeen, and my oldest brother, Charles, joined the army at eighteen. That made me the oldest girl at home for a long time.

The picture above shows Charles in his first year of service. The picture on the left is of my other big brother, John.

While my brothers did the outside chores, the girls in my family were responsible for running the household. I always heard from my mom and dad, "You are responsible for these kids." I had to learn to keep house, cook, manage people, and be bossy. My mom worked as a nurse, and my dad was a porter on a train. I would get into trouble if a chore wasn't done when they came home from work.

I learned to iron at age six and was

making whole meals for my family by age twelve. In the picture on the left, I was fifteen and had been helping to take care of my family for nine years.

A Different Kitchen

The kitchen I cooked in looked quite different from yours. No one in our neighborhood had a refrigerator. Most families used an icebox, a large cabinet that held a huge chunk of ice to keep it cool. As the ice melted, a pan at the bottom of the icebox caught the dripping water.

The iceman came to our house every day in the summer to see if we needed any ice to keep our icebox cool. We usually bought a twenty-five-pound block. He would pull the ice chunk from the back of the delivery truck with huge tongs and bring it into our house.

    Instead of using a gas or electric stove, we heated our
water and did all our cooking on a wood-burning stove with
four big burners. Two smaller burners were off to one side.
The stove had a small compartment where we could keep
food warm. Below the burners on one side was a big oven
for baking. The whole stove was made of cast iron. We had
to polish it with a special polish called blacking.

 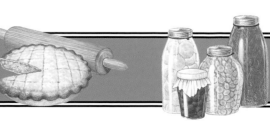

Rationing for War

When I was growing up, the United States fought in a war called World War II. In order for the people fighting in the war to have enough food and other goods, the government limited what families could buy through rationing. People were given coupon books with coupons for various products. When we went to the store, we needed to bring our coupon books and enough money to buy what we wanted. With eleven kids in our family, we got plenty of ration coupons for food. We had so many coupons for sugar that my mother used to sell our extra ones to our neighbors and friends.

Where our men are fighting

OUR FOOD IS FIGHTING

BUY WISELY – COOK CAREFULLY – STORE CAREFULLY – USE LEFTOVERS

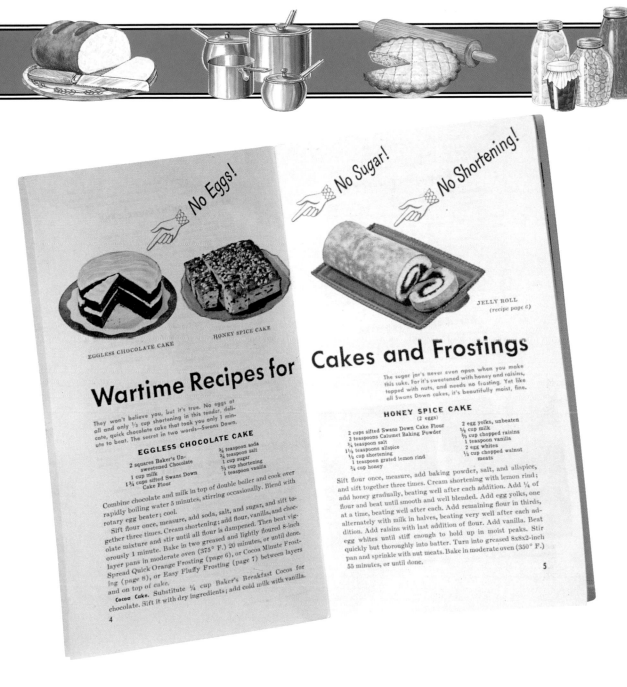

No Eggs!

No Sugar!

No Shortening!

JELLY ROLL
(recipe page 6)

EGGLESS CHOCOLATE CAKE

HONEY SPICE CAKE

Wartime Recipes for Cakes and Frostings

They won't believe you, but it's true. No eggs at all and only ⅓ cup shortening in this tender, delicate, quick chocolate cake that took you only 1 minute to beat. The secret in two words—Swans Down.

The sugar jar's never even open when you make this cake. For it's sweetened with honey and raisins, topped with nuts, and needs no frosting. Yet like all Swans Down cakes, it's beautifully moist, fine.

EGGLESS CHOCOLATE CAKE

2 squares Baker's Unsweetened Chocolate
1 cup milk
1¾ cups sifted Swans Down Cake Flour

¾ teaspoon soda
½ teaspoon salt
1 cup sugar
⅓ cup shortening
1 teaspoon vanilla

Combine chocolate and milk in top of double boiler and cook over rapidly boiling water 5 minutes, stirring occasionally. Blend with rotary egg beater; cool.

Sift flour once, measure, add soda, salt, and sugar, and sift together three times. Cream shortening; add flour, vanilla, and chocolate mixture and stir until all flour is dampened. Then beat vigorously 1 minute. Bake in two greased and lightly floured 8-inch layer pans in moderate oven (375° F.) 20 minutes, or until done. Spread Quick Orange Frosting (page 6), or Cocoa Minute Frosting (page 8), or Easy Fluffy Frosting (page 7) between layers and on top of cake.

Cocoa Cake. Substitute ¼ cup Baker's Breakfast Cocoa for chocolate. Sift it with dry ingredients; add cold milk with vanilla.

4

HONEY SPICE CAKE
(2 eggs)

2 cups sifted Swans Down Cake Flour
2 teaspoons Calumet Baking Powder
¾ teaspoon salt
1½ teaspoons allspice
⅓ cup shortening
1 teaspoon grated lemon rind
¾ cup honey

2 egg yolks, unbeaten
¼ cup milk
⅔ cup chopped raisins
1 teaspoon vanilla
2 egg whites
½ cup chopped walnut meats

Sift flour once, measure, add baking powder, salt, and allspice, and sift together three times. Cream shortening with lemon rind; add honey gradually, beating well after each addition. Add ¼ of flour and beat until smooth and well blended. Add egg yolks, one at a time, beating well after each. Add remaining flour in thirds, alternately with milk in halves, beating very well after each addition. Add raisins with last addition of flour. Add vanilla. Beat egg whites until stiff enough to hold up in moist peaks. Stir quickly but thoroughly into batter. Turn into greased 8x8x2-inch pan and sprinkle with nut meats. Bake in moderate oven (350° F.) 55 minutes, or until done.

5

There were special wartime cookbooks that had recipes for all sorts of meals and desserts that could be made without rationed ingredients.

During the war, extra food was needed to feed the soldiers. The U.S. government asked people to plant their own vegetable gardens to add to the country's food supply. These vegetable gardens were known as "victory gardens" because they helped our country win the war. People dug victory gardens in their backyards and anywhere else there

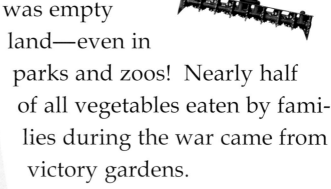

was empty land—even in parks and zoos! Nearly half of all vegetables eaten by families during the war came from victory gardens.

PLANT A VICTORY GARDEN

OUR FOOD IS FIGHTING

A GARDEN WILL MAKE YOUR RATIONS GO FURTHER

Though we didn't have a victory garden, many of our neighbors did. They grew tomatoes, greens, cucumbers, and onions. We got our produce from the store or a nearby farm.

HAVE A

Victory Garden

Eat what you can, and can what you can't eat

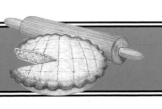

Canning: A Family Event

On Friday evenings, my dad would sometimes take the truck to the farms just outside of town. He'd come back with baskets of vegetables—tomatoes, string beans, or beets. Sometimes we went with him to pick peaches. Then all weekend, my mom, my grandmother, and all the kids would can this produce. Sometimes neighbors would come and help, and we kids could go play while they worked.

My job was to wash the jars and lids. A grown-up always put my clean jars in boiling water to sterilize them, then set them upside down on a clean cloth to cool. We packed the jars with uncooked vegetables, pushing the vegetables down with a big spoon. Then we screwed the lids tightly onto the jars. My mom put the filled jars in a big pot with a rack to hold them in place. Boiling water covered the tops of the jars.

We could hear the lids popping as they sealed. If a lid didn't pop, we knew the jar hadn't sealed and we would have to eat the beans the next day. We canned forty to fifty jars a day, working until nine o'clock at night.

Storing the Fruits of Summer

In the late summer and early fall, the older kids had to help my grandma make jam. She used peaches, grapes, apples, and plums. We washed whatever fruit we had and put it into a huge iron pot on the wood-burning stove.

We boiled the fruit until it got mushy. Then we squeezed it through a sieve and combined the juice that came out with sugar and pectin, which made it thick.

My grandmother would scold us as we kept putting our fingers in the jam and licking them. Thick, sticky fruit covered our faces. Sweet smells of cooking fruit drifted through the house and out into the backyard.

We put the cooled jam in glass jars, covered the tops with paraffin (a kind of wax), and screwed on the metal lids. That helped keep the jam fresh. The whole process was called "putting up jam."

With my mom's canned vegetables and my grandmother's jam, the shelves in our cupboards were always well stocked.

Breakfast

Every morning, we awoke to the smell of fresh coffee drifting through the duplex. There were no electric coffeemakers in those days. My mother brewed our Marvel coffee in a tall aluminum coffeepot on the back of the stove. I loved the smell but could never learn to like the taste, even as a grown-up.

There were no microwave ovens then, either. People really had to plan their meals because there was no way to heat up something quickly. So my mom often started breakfast and dinner at the same time. She would put a roast or a chicken in the oven and cook it while we were eating breakfast.

We usually had hot farina, oat-meal, or All-Bran for breakfast. On weekends, we could have bacon, eggs, and potatoes with fried onions. It was all so tasty! Sometimes my mother would make her delicious homemade biscuits for breakfast.

She also liked to make hot rolls or corn bread. We would heap my grand-mother's jam on my mom's homemade breads. I did not know about store-bought bread until I was in high school!

There were no school lunch programs then, so after a morning at school, we all walked home for a big lunch. My mom came home from work to eat, too.

We often had a delicious stew or meat loaf with mashed potatoes and corn bread, made by my grandmother. My favorite meal was beef roast with potatoes and carrots in beef gravy.

MARVEL BRAND

COUNTRY GENTLEMAN SWEET CORN

WHITE CREAM STYLE
CONTENTS 1 LB. 4 OZS.

My grandmother always served a vegetable, like green beans, okra, or corn. Back then, there were no freezers in homes or in many stores, so through much of the year we ate canned vegetables. In the summer and early fall, we ate fresh vegetables.

SILVER LAKE BRAND U.S.A

TOMATOES
CONTENTS 6 LBS. 5 OZ.

At every meal, we drank milk or water. And of course, there was always homemade pudding or pie for dessert. I especially loved my grandmother's banana pudding. Pudding mixes, frozen pie crusts, canned pie fillings, and whipped cream in spray cans had not been invented yet.

After lunch, we went back to school, which let out at three-thirty. Right after we got home, we got out of our school clothes and into our play clothes and did homework. All our homework had to be done before dinner.

We rarely had snacks after school. Peanut butter on crackers, cookies, or animal crackers were a luxury. We never drank soda, and very few kinds of juice were available.

24

We always ate dinner as a family as soon as my parents got home from work, about four-thirty or five o'clock. I was often responsible for making dinner, which was much like our big lunch, and my brothers and sisters had to help my mom clean the kitchen afterward. The kids took turns cleaning our huge stainless-steel pots, which always gleamed.

Neighborhood Shopping

With so many children, we bought food in large quantities. My grandmother cooked with huge amounts of food, as though she were working in a restaurant. We bought flour and sugar in one hundred-pound sacks and potatoes and onions in fifty-pound sacks.

In those days, there were very few supermarkets. Small grocery stores and butcher shops stood on many corners.

Like many families in our neighborhood, we didn't have a car to drive to the store. When my mom needed something, she would send my brothers down to the grocery store on the corner. "Tell Mr. Adolph to send me a bag of potatoes," she would say.

Mr. Adolph would mark the cost of the potatoes on a bill for my parents to pay later, kind of like the way your parents use a credit card. Then my brothers would head for home, pulling the wagon loaded with food behind them. Families who had telephones could order their groceries over the phone and have a delivery boy bring the food to their homes.

COPYRIGHT 1925 BY KIDD & CO., Inc.

Kidd's Peanut Brittle CANDY

NET WEIGHT ONE POUND
MADE BY
KIDD & CO. INC.
CHICAGO ILLINOIS

Homemade Treats

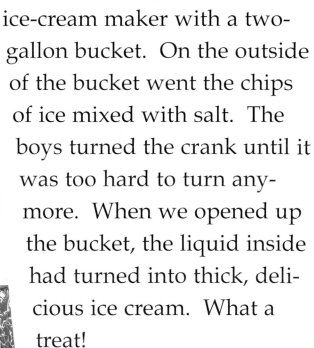

On Sundays, we would sometimes make homemade ice cream. It was one of our favorite treats. We cooked a mixture of sugar, eggs, canned evaporated milk, and whatever flavoring we wanted—vanilla, strawberries, or peaches—until it boiled and thickened. Then we strained it through a loosely woven cotton cloth called cheesecloth.

Once the milk mixture was cool, we would pour it into an

ice-cream maker with a two-gallon bucket. On the outside of the bucket went the chips of ice mixed with salt. The boys turned the crank until it was too hard to turn anymore. When we opened up the bucket, the liquid inside had turned into thick, delicious ice cream. What a treat!

My mom liked to make popcorn for us to eat while we listened to the shows on the radio. She would heat oil in a big pan on the stove. When the oil was hot enough, she'd pour in the popcorn. Mom had to keep shaking the pan to make sure the kernels didn't burn as they popped.

The foods we eat and the way we cook may have changed since I was a child, but one thing is the same: I still enjoy making food with my family and sitting down together to enjoy a meal. It brings us all closer as a family.

Glossary

blacking: a polish that is rubbed on an object such as a stove to make it black

farina: a finely ground grain made into cereal

icebox: a cabinet that keeps food cool with a large block of ice

lard: a soft, white fat used in cooking. Lard comes from pigs.

paraffin: a kind of wax used in canning to seal food in jars

pectin: a substance made from fruit that is used to thicken jams and jellies

porter: a person who waits on people in passenger trains

rationing: limiting to fixed portions. When certain items are scarce, the government sometimes limits how many of these items people can buy.

sieve: a round bowl of metal or plastic that has many holes in it to sift or drain ingredients

tongs: a tool with two connected curved arms that pick up things

victory gardens: vegetable gardens planted across the United States during World War II to increase the country's food supply

For Further Reading

Duden, Jane. *Timeline: 1940s.* New York: Crestwood House, 1989.

Mack-Williams, Kibibi. *Food and Our History.* Vero Beach, Fla.: Roarke Press, 1995.

Rubel, David. *The United States in the 20th Century.* New York: Scholastic, 1995.

Stein, R. Conrad. *The Home Front.* Chicago: Children's Press, 1986.

Trotter, Joe Williams, Jr. *From a Raw Deal to a New Deal? African Americans, 1929-1945.* New York: Oxford University Press, 1996.

Whitman, Sylvia. *V Is for Victory: The American Home Front during World War II.* Minneapolis, Minn.: Lerner Publications Co., 1993.

Index

biscuits, 6, 21
bread, 21
bread pudding, 6, 7
breakfast, 20–21
butcher shops, 26

canning, 16–17, 18, 19, 22
cereal, 21
chores, 9, 25
coffee, 20
cookbooks, 13
cooking, 5, 6, 7, 11, 13, 20, 25
corn bread, 21

deliveries, 27
desserts, 6, 7, 23, 28
dinner, 20, 25
drinks, 23, 24

families, big, 5
farina, 21
fruit, 16, 18, 28

grocery stores, 26

iceboxes, 10
ice cream, 28

jam, 18, 19, 21

kitchens, 10–11

lunch, 22

oatmeal, 21

popcorn, 29

ration coupons, 12
rationing, 12–13
refrigerators, 10

school, 22, 24
shopping, 26–27
snacks, 24, 29
stoves, 11

vegetables, 14, 15, 16, 22
victory gardens, 14–15

wood-burning stoves, 11